Fingerpower®

Level Three

Effective Technic for All Piano Methods

By John W. Schaum

Edited by Wesley Schaum

FOREWORD

Strong fingers are an important requirement for all pianists, amateur and professional. Schaum Fingerpower® exercises are designed to strengthen all five fingers of both hands. Equal hand development is assured by the performance of the same patterns in each hand.

The exercises are short and easily memorized. This enables the student to focus his/her efforts on technical benefits, listening attentively and playing with a steady beat.

A measure number (enclosed in a small box) is included at the beginning of each system of music. This makes it easier to locate measures during the lesson and for written practice assignments.

The exercises become progressively more difficult as the student moves through the book. This makes the exercises an ideal companion to a method book at the same level.

The series consists of seven books, Primer Level through Level 6.

Practice CD's and MIDI diskettes with orchestrated accompaniments are available for this book. They promote accurate playing with a steady rhythm, while making practice more enjoyable. MIDI diskettes have separate tracks for right hand, left hand, harmony, bass and rhythm.

Practice CD (catalog No. 04-23cd) – **MIDI Diskette** (catalog No. 04-23md)

Schaum Publications, Inc. • 10235 N. Port Washington Rd. • Mequon, WI 53092 • www.schaumpiano.net

ISBN-13: 978-1-936098-09-5

04-23

CONTENTS

PRACTICE SUGGESTIONS

To derive the full benefit from these exercises, they should be played with a firm, solid finger action. Try to play each finger equally loud. Each hand should also play equally loud. This may requre extra practice in the weaker hand. Listen carefully while practicing. It is also important to be aware of the feeling in your fingers and hands during practice.

Each exercise should be practiced four or five times daily, starting at a slow tempo and gradually increasing the speed as proficiency improves. Several previously learned exercises should be reviewed each week as part of regular practice.

For Level Three supplements, books and sheet music, see our web site:
www.schaumpiano.net

1. Triplets

CD 1/2   MIDI 1

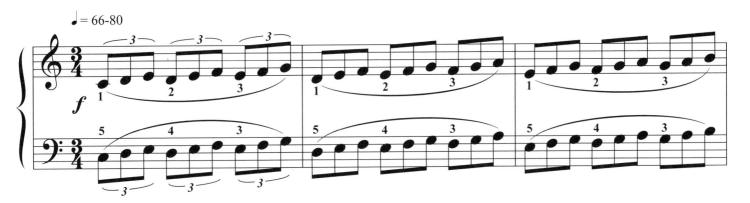

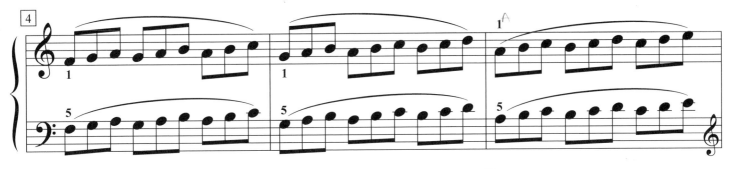

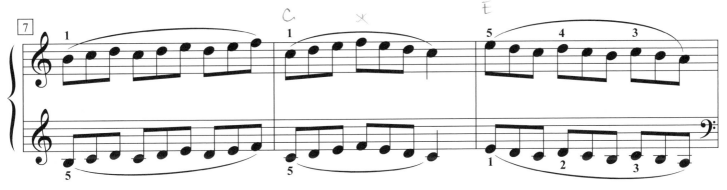

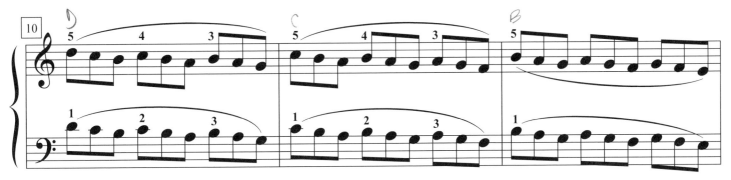

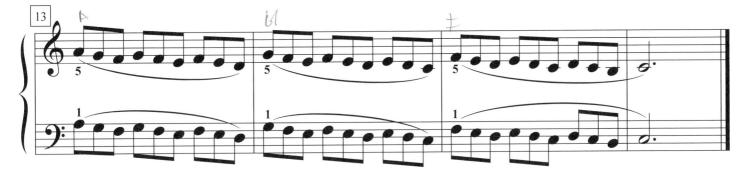

2. Two Notes Against One (R.H.)

CD 3/4   MIDI 2

♩ = 92-104

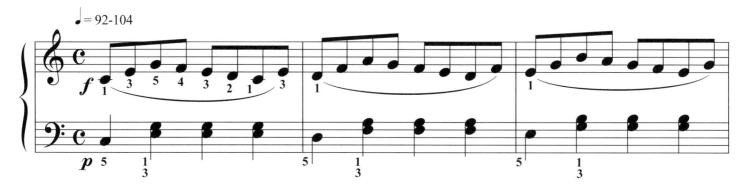

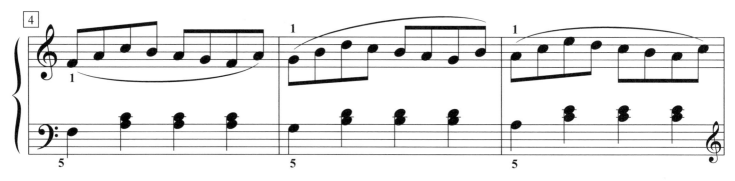

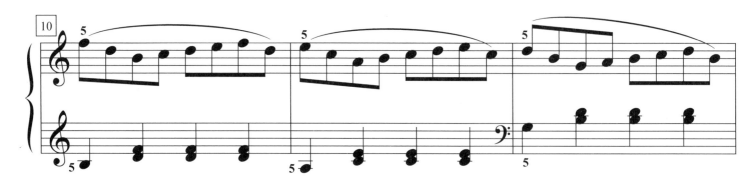

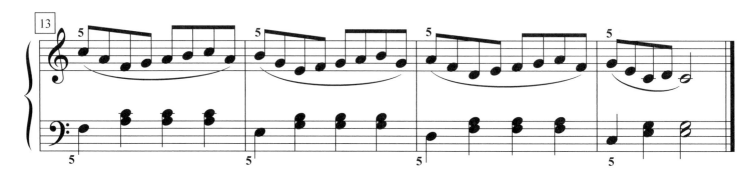

3. Two Notes Against One (L.H.)

CD 5/6   MIDI 3

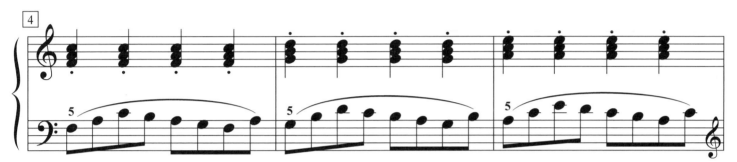

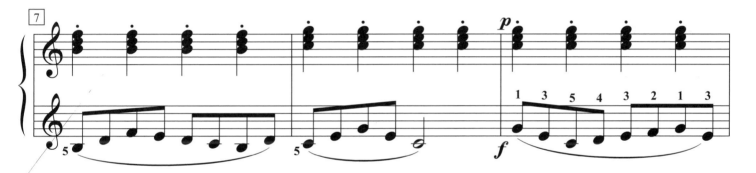

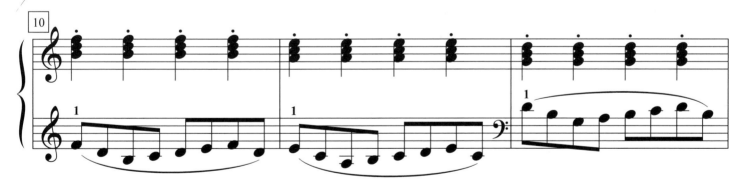

4. Cross Hand Etude (3/4)

CD 7/8   MIDI 4

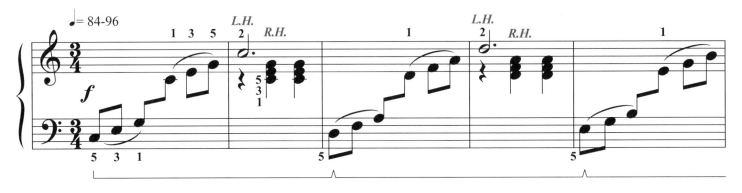

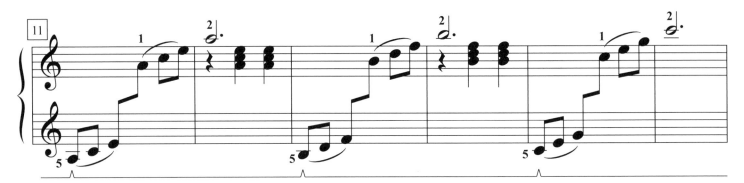

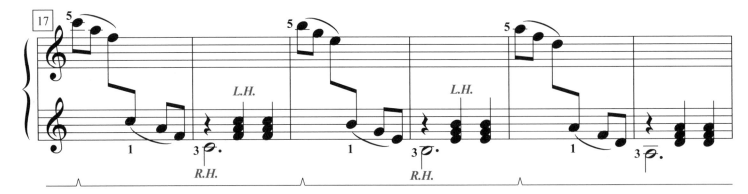

5. Cross Hand Etude (4/4)

CD 9/10   MIDI 5

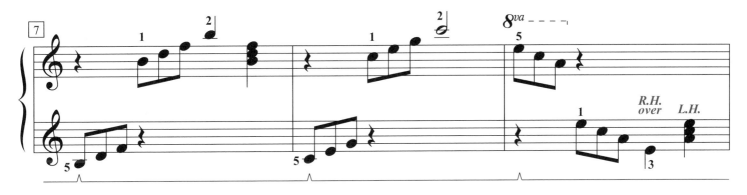

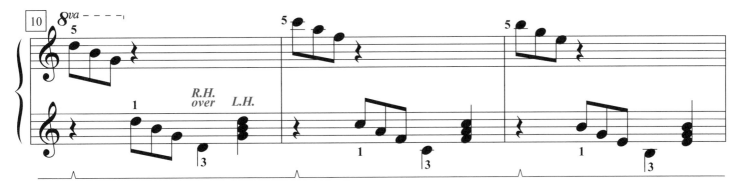

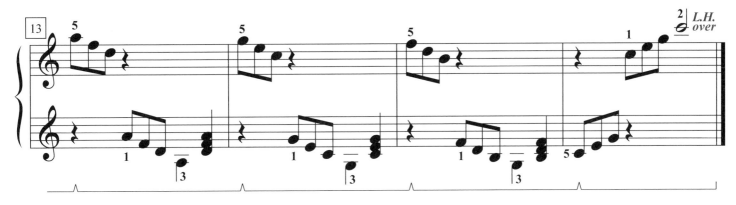

6. Chord Inversions

CD 11/12   MIDI 6

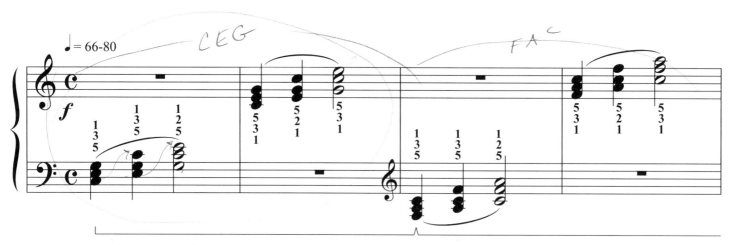

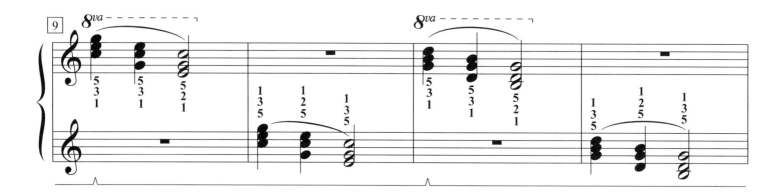

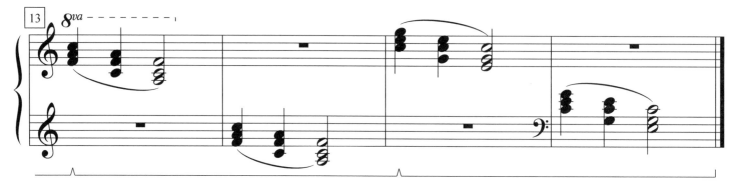

*8va = play one octave HIGHER than written.

7. Hand Stretching Technique

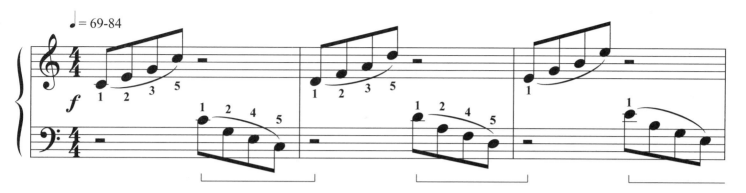

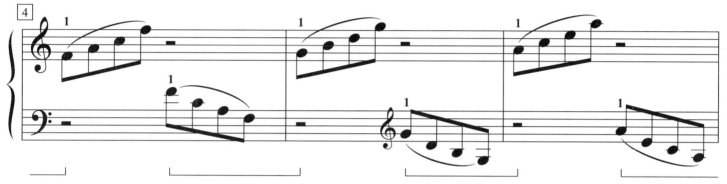

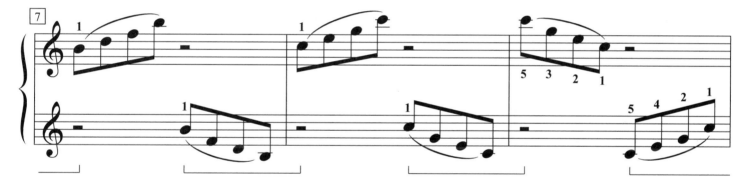

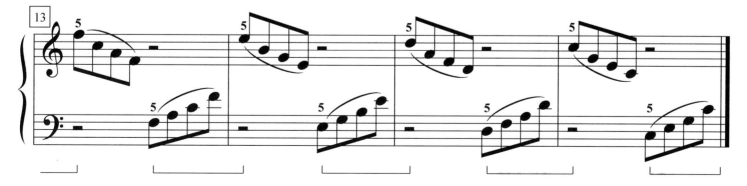

8. Finger Velocity

CD 15/16   MIDI 8

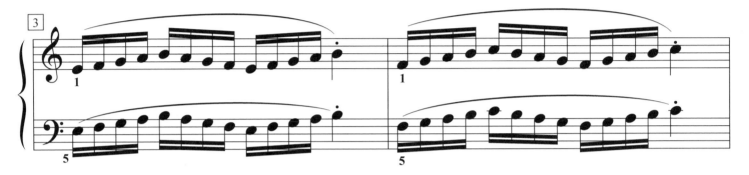

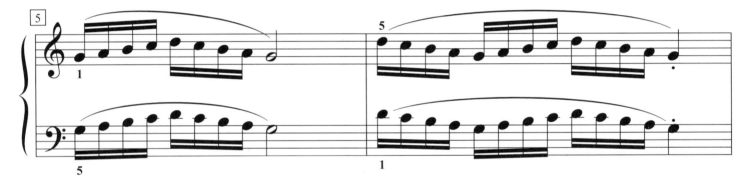

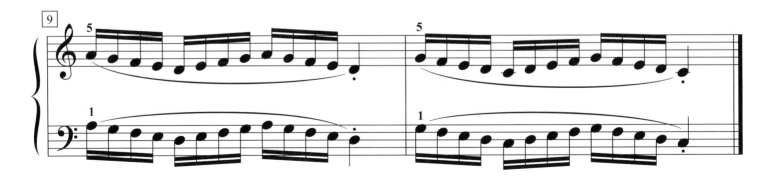

*9. Sustaining the Thumb

CD 17/18   MIDI 9

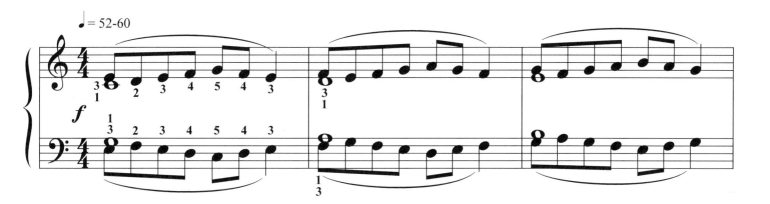

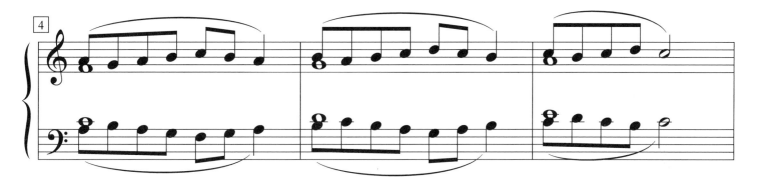

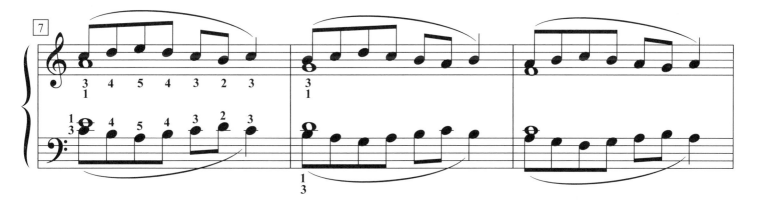

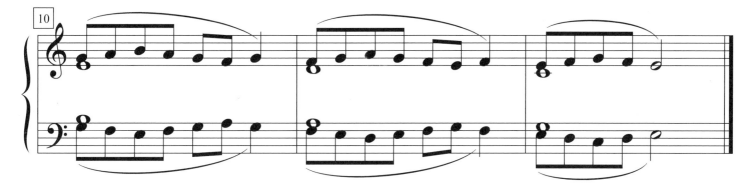

* Be sure that all whole notes played by the thumb are held down for *four full counts*.

*10. Sustaining the Second Finger

CD 19/20   MIDI 10

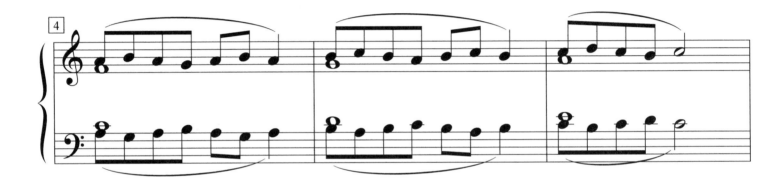

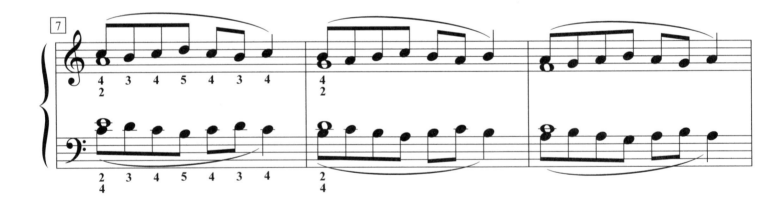

* Be sure that all whole notes played by the 2nd finger are held down for *four full counts*.

*11. Sustaining the Third Finger

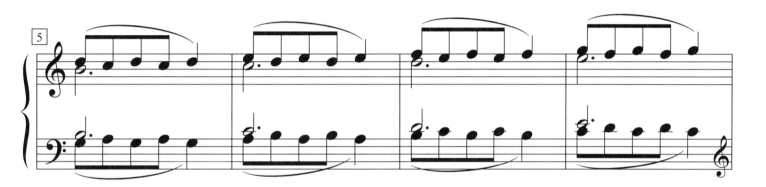

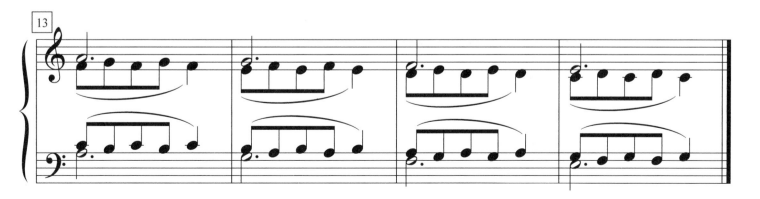

* Be sure that all dotted half notes played by the 3rd finger are held down for *three full counts.*

*12. Sustaining the Fourth Finger

CD 23/24   MIDI 12

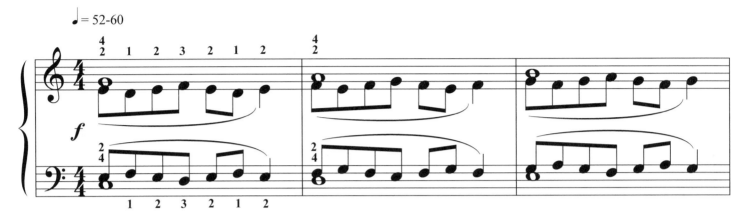

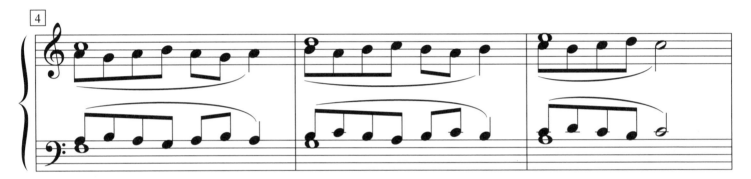

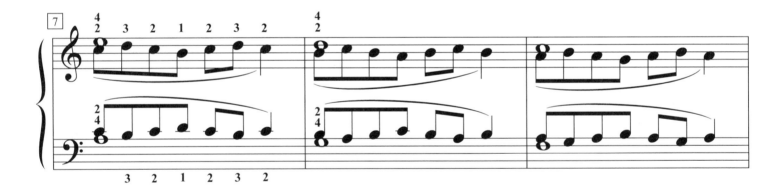

* Be sure that all whole notes played by the 4th finger are held down for *four full counts.*

*13. Sustaining the Fifth Finger

CD 25/26   MIDI 13

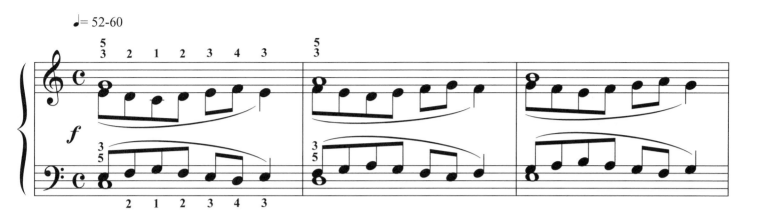

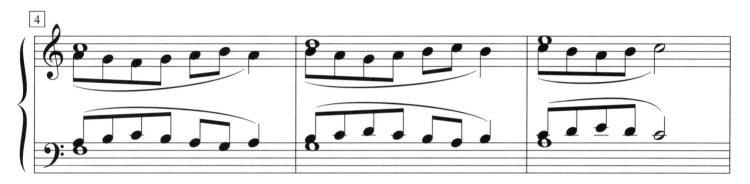

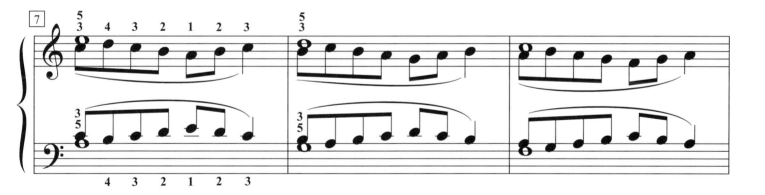

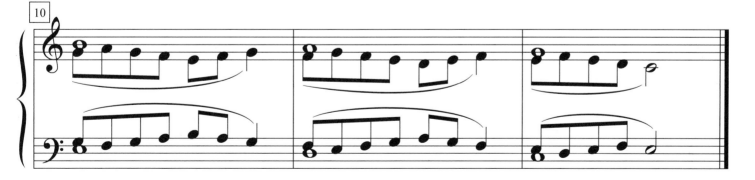

* Be sure that all whole notes played by the 5th finger are held down for *four full counts.*

14. Scale Passages and Staccato Chords

CD 27/28   MIDI 14

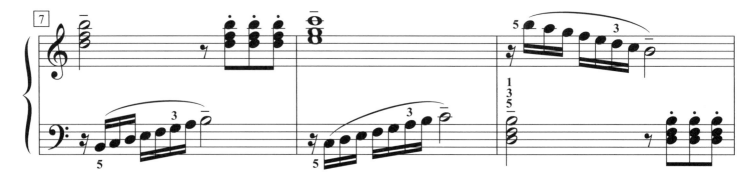

15. Legato Thirds

CD 29/30   MIDI 15

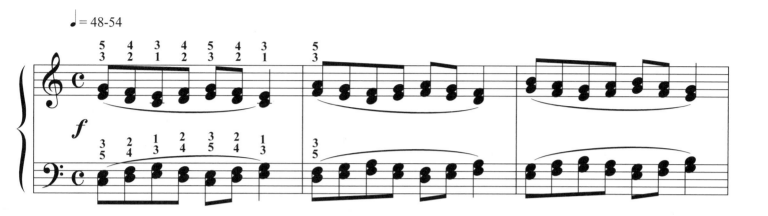

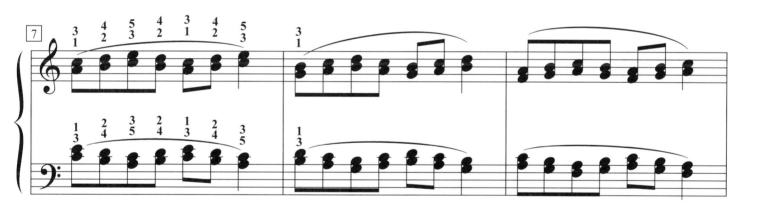

*16. Dotted Eighth and Sixteenth Notes

CD 31/32   MIDI 16

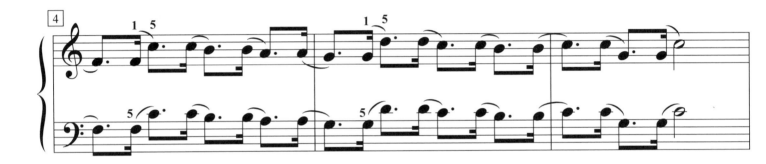

* The rhythm for the dotted 8th and 16th must be **played accurately**. Be careful that it is **not** played like an 8th note triplet.

17. Etude For the Weaker Fingers

CD 33/34   MIDI 17

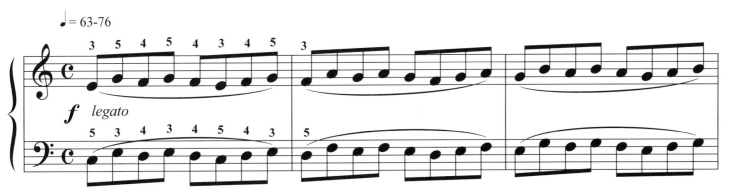

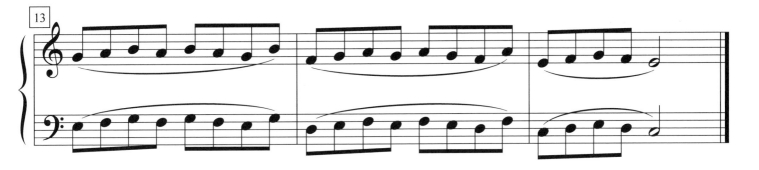

18. Interlocking Hand Pattern

CD 35/36   MIDI 18

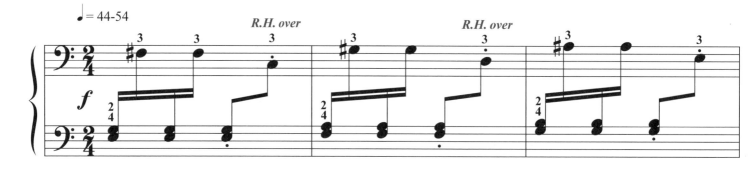

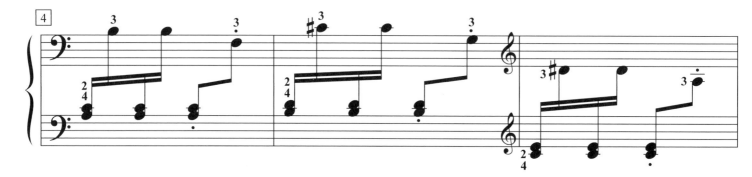

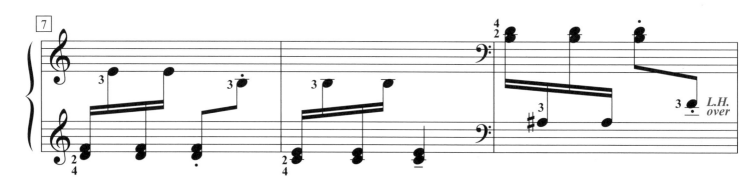

19. Chromatic Chord Etude

CD 37/38   MIDI 19

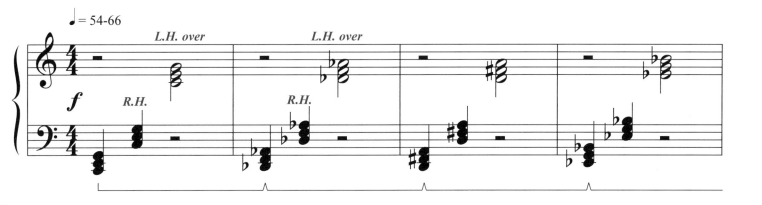

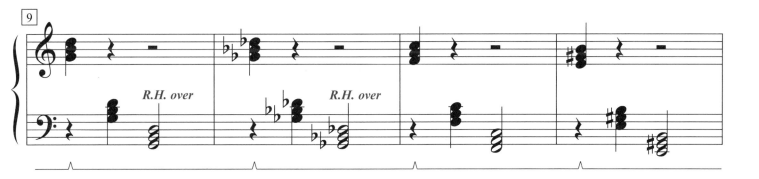

20. Chromatic Arpeggio Etude

CD 39/40   MIDI 20

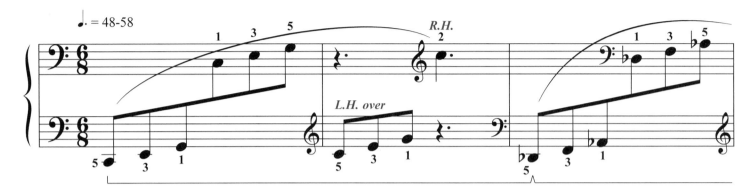

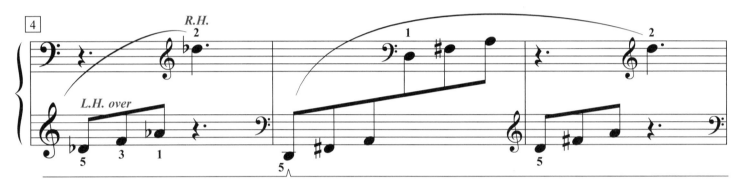

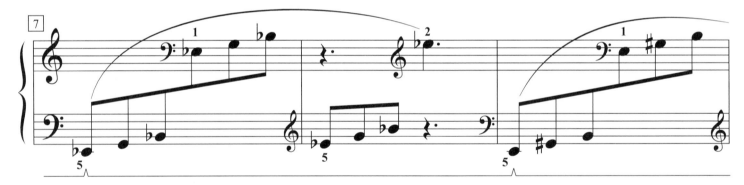

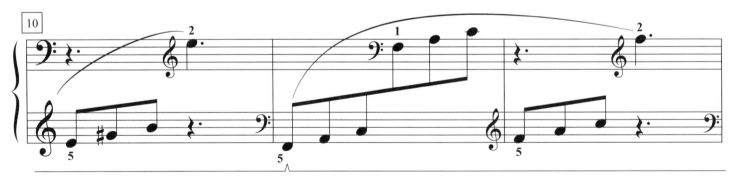

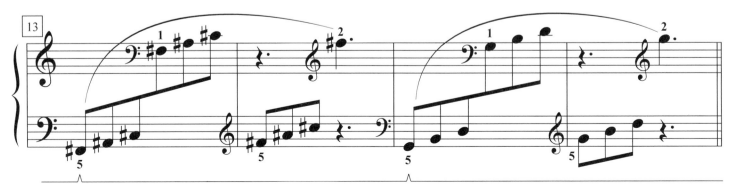

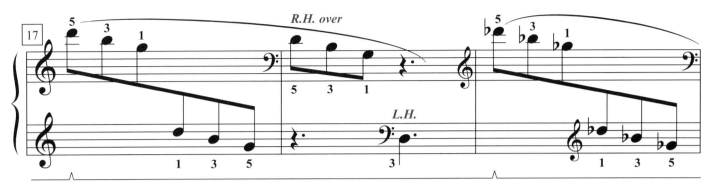

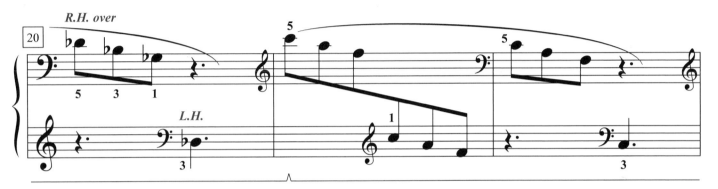

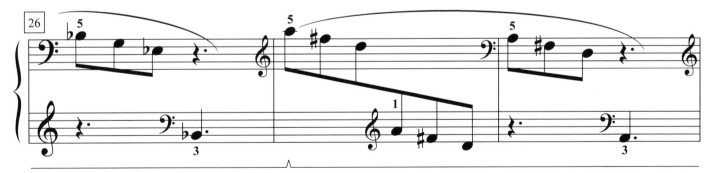

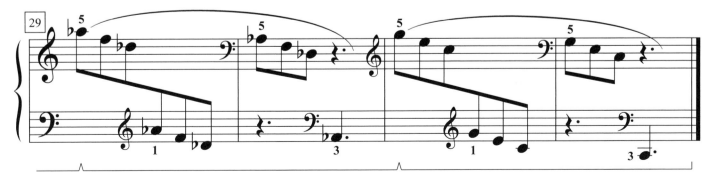

Reference Page

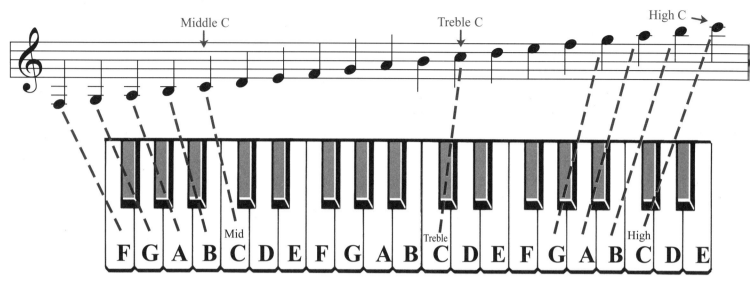

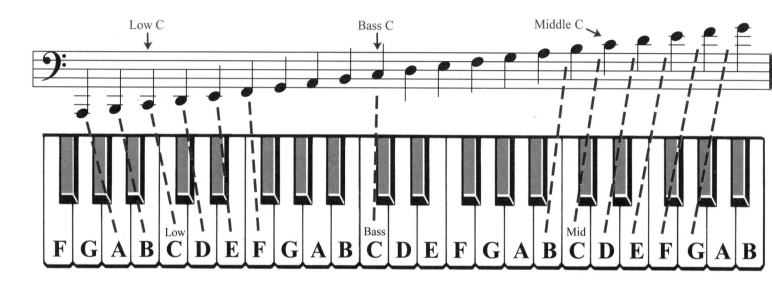

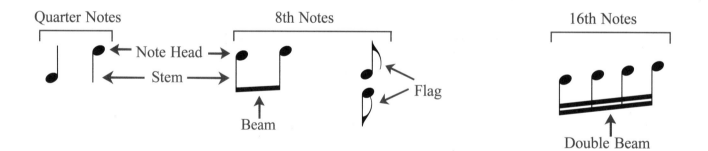

Quarter Notes   8th Notes   16th Notes

Note Head

Stem

Beam

Flag

Double Beam

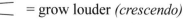 = small accent

> = medium accent

ʌ = big accent

= grow louder (*crescendo*)

= get softer (*diminuendo*)

ff = very loud (*fortissimo*)

f = loud (*forte*)

mf = medium loud (*mezzo forte*)

mp = medium soft (*mezzo piano*)

p = soft (*piano*)

pp = very soft (*pianissimo*)